Hi, I'm Bird!

Hello, I'm Bee!

A NOTE TO PARENTS, TEACHERS, LIBRARIANS, CAREGIVERS,
HEALTH PROFESSIONALS, CLERGY, AND ALL THOSE WHO SPEND
TIME WITH, CARE FOR, OR WORK WITH YOUNG CHILDREN

Our young children are curious about almost everything. They are especially
curious about their bodies, about where they came from, and how they were
made. Many, but not all, ask us endless questions about these topics. They ask us
why their bodies are the same and different from other people's bodies, what
makes a girl a girl and a boy a boy, what the names are of all the different parts of
their bodies, where babies come from, how babies are made, what a family is —
and so many other questions about themselves and their bodies. Many of their
questions are easy to answer. Others are more difficult to answer.

We created this book to answer young children's many questions and concerns
about these issues. We talked with parents, teachers, librarians, nurses, doctors,
social workers, psychologists, scientists, health professionals, and clergy to make
sure that all the material in this book is age-appropriate, scientifically accurate, and,
at this time, as up-to-date as possible. Many have asked us how best to use this
book with children. There is no one answer. This book can be used as a shared
experience between a child and an adult. Some children may want the book read to
them from cover to cover. Other children may pick only the part or parts that
interest them or answer a specific question they may have. And others may wish to
look through or read the book on their own.

No matter which way our book is used, it is our hope that it will help answer
young children's perfectly normal and amazing questions about their bodies, about
where they came from, and about what makes them either a boy or a girl.

—Robie H. Harris and Michael Emberley, January 2006

It's NOT the Stork!

A Book About Girls, Boys, Babies, Bodies, Families, and Friends

Robie H. Harris   illustrated by Michael Emberley

CANDLEWICK PRESS

Contents

I can't WAIT to find out about ALL this stuff!

I CAN wait. . . .

Let's go to the zoo and see the hippos!

I can't WAIT to go and see the insects!

BEES

Bird and Bee Go to the Zoo

Babies are everywhere!

Families are everywhere!

1

So-ooo Many Questions!

You've probably seen all kinds of families—your own family, or a cousin's, or friend's or neighbor's family —or a dog or cat, penguin, pig, hippo, horse, dolphin, or elephant family— cuddling, loving, feeding, caring for, and playing with their babies.

Baby birds chirping are the cutest babies of all!

Baby bees buzzing are the cutest babies of all!

You may have a lot of questions about where all these babies come from—or where you came from—or how you were made—or how you were born.

I come from Ipswich. It's a town. That's where I come from.

I come from Buffalo. It's a city. That's where I come from.

You may also wonder about what makes a baby a girl or a boy—or how girls and boys are the same and how they are different.

Asking questions is a great way to find out about lots of things. Asking a grownup—your mommy, your daddy, or aunt, uncle, or grandparent, or your nurse or doctor—is a great way to find answers to your questions.

Looking through a book on your own, or asking your teacher or librarian or someone you know well to read a book to you, are other great ways to find answers.

Girls Do This, Boys Do That

Same?
Different?

Most parts of people's bodies are the same—our toes, our fingers, our noses, our legs, our arms, our eyes, our hearts, our lungs, our stomachs, our buttocks—and many other parts too.

But some of the private parts people are born with are not the same. The vagina and the penis are two of these private parts that are not the same.

Some of our private parts are on the OUTSIDE of our bodies. They are the parts that are usually covered by underpants, or a bathing suit, or for babies and little kids—a diaper.

Some of our private parts are INSIDE our bodies. But we cannot see the INSIDE parts with our own eyes.

Another thing that's different about boys and men and girls and women is how they use the toilet. That's because some parts of their bodies are different. Pee comes out through a small opening at the tip of boys' and men's penises. Pee comes out through a small opening between girls' and women's legs.

That's why girls and women sit on the toilet when they pee, and why boys and men usually stand up when they pee. One thing that is the same for boys and men and girls and women is that they all sit on the toilet when they poop.

One more thing that's different is that baby girls, girls, and women are called "females," and baby boys, boys, and men are called "males."

15

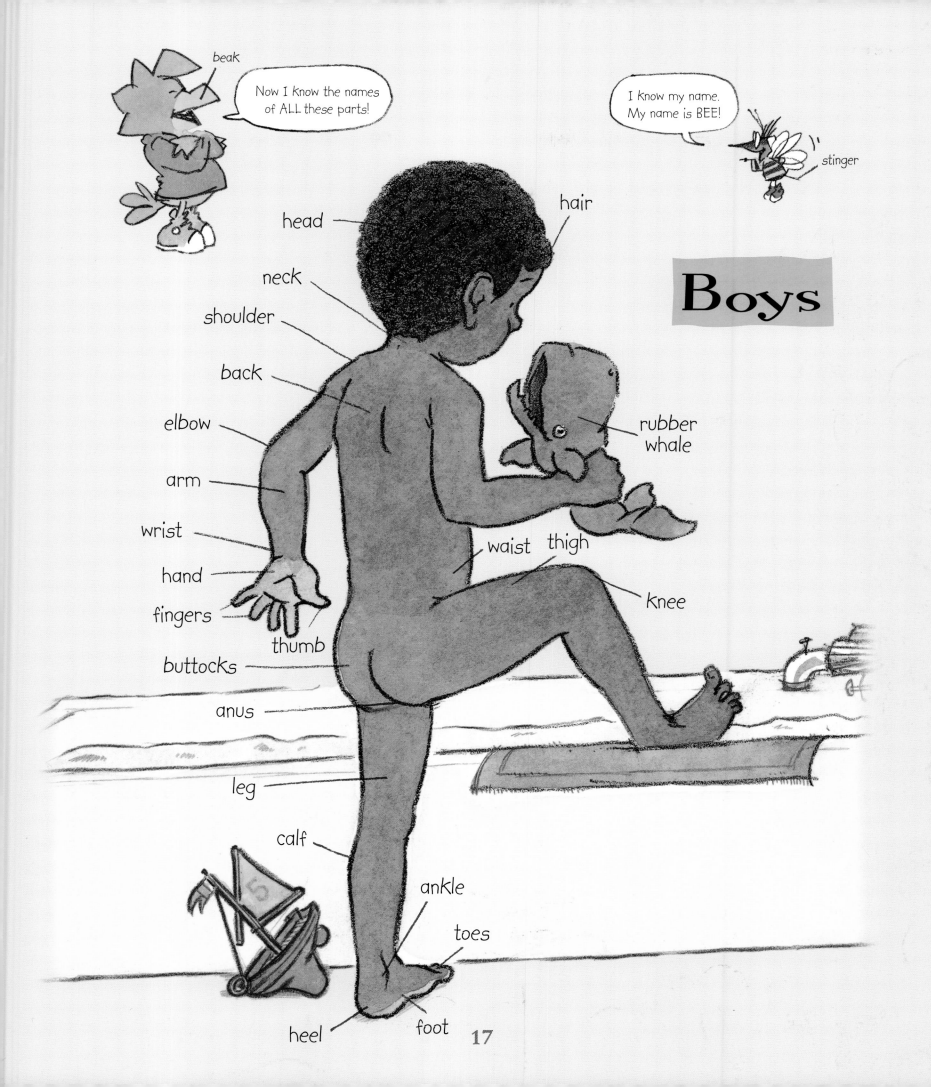

Head to Toe

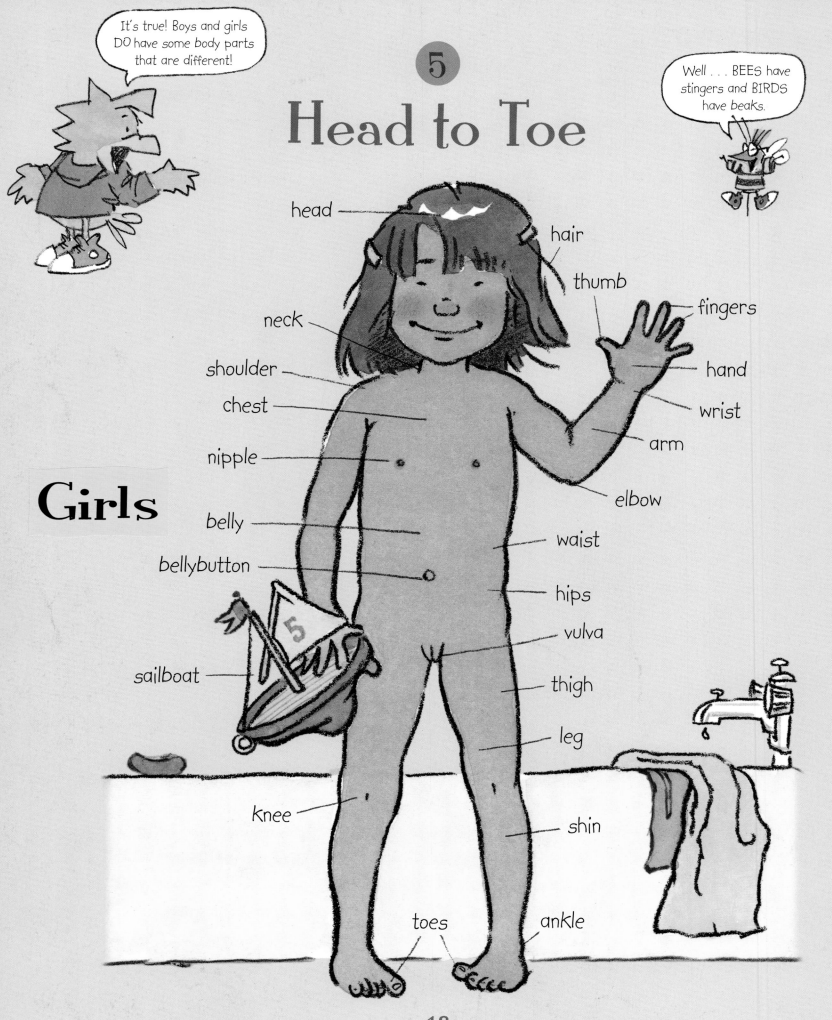

Boys

What Boys Have

Yikes! Baby boys, boys, and men have the same special body parts?

Yep! And bees and birds have wings!

Baby boys are born with some special body parts that baby girls are not born with. Some of these parts are on the outside of the body and some are inside the body.

The special OUTSIDE parts—the penis and the scrotum—hang between boys' and men's legs. That's why they are easy to see. Girls and women do not have these parts.

Two other OUTSIDE parts—the opening to the urethra and the anus—are also between boys' and men's legs. Girls and women have these parts too.

The SCROTUM is a soft bag of squishy skin that holds the two testicles.

The PENIS hangs in front of the scrotum. Sometimes, penises get hard and stick out. That's called "having an erection." Baby boys, boys, and men all have erections. Baby boys even have erections before they are born, while they are growing inside their mothers' bodies. The small opening at the end of the penis—where pee comes out—is called the OPENING TO THE URETHRA.

Poop, also called "b.m.," comes out of an opening called the ANUS.

Boys and men have two openings between their legs—the opening at the tip of the penis and the anus.

penis

opening to the urethra

scrotum

anus

The special parts INSIDE boys' and men's bodies are the two testicles and the two vas deferens tubes. Girls and women do not have these two parts.

Two other parts—the bladder and the urethra—are also INSIDE boys and men's bodies. Girls and women have these parts too.

A young boy's two TESTICLES are each about the size of a grape. Two small tubes—the VAS DEFERENS—look like strands of cooked spaghetti.

Pee comes from the BLADDER and goes into a small tube inside the penis called the URETHRA. Pee leaves boys' and men's bodies through the small opening at the end of the penis.

The loose skin at the end of the penis is called the "foreskin." Some baby boys' foreskins are removed a few days after they are born. Some baby boys' foreskins are not removed. That's why some penises look different from other penises.

bladder

urethra

vas deferens tubes

penis

testicle

testicle

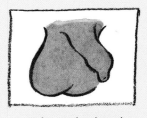

uncircumcised penis
penis with a foreskin

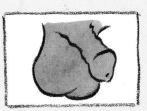

circumcised penis
penis without a foreskin

What Girls Have

Yikes! Baby girls, girls, and women have the same special body parts?

Yep! And bees and birds have legs!

Baby girls are born with some special body parts that baby boys are not born with. Some of these parts are on the outside of the body and some are inside the body.

The special OUTSIDE parts—the vulva, the opening to the vagina, and the clitoris—are between girls' and women's legs. That's why they are hard to see. Boys and men do not have these parts.

Two other OUTSIDE parts—the opening to the urethra and the anus—are also between girls' and women's legs. Boys and men have these parts too.

The VULVA is the area of soft skin between girls' and women's legs.

Inside the vulva is a small bump of skin, about the size of a pea, called the CLITORIS. Also inside the vulva are two small openings—the OPENING TO THE URETHRA, where pee comes out—and the OPENING TO THE VAGINA.

Poop, also called "b.m.," comes out of an opening called the ANUS.

Girls and women have three openings between their legs—the opening to the urethra, the opening to the vagina, and the anus.

clitoris

opening to the urethra

opening to the vagina

vulva

anus

The special parts INSIDE girls' and women's bodies are the two ovaries, the two Fallopian tubes, the uterus, and the vagina. Boys and men do not have these parts.

Two other parts—the bladder and the urethra—are also INSIDE girls' and women's bodies. Boys and men have these parts, too.

A young girl's two OVARIES are each about the size of a grape.

The two FALLOPIAN TUBES are about as narrow as soda straws.

The VAGINA is a stretchy tube that goes from the uterus to the outside of the body.

A young girl's UTERUS is about the size of a small plum.

Pee comes from the BLADDER and goes into a small tube called the URETHRA. Pee leaves girls' and women's bodies through the small opening at the end of the urethra.

Fallopian tubes

ovary

ovary

uterus

bladder

vagina

urethra

Knowing the names of ALL the parts of your body is—

PERFECTLY NORMAL!

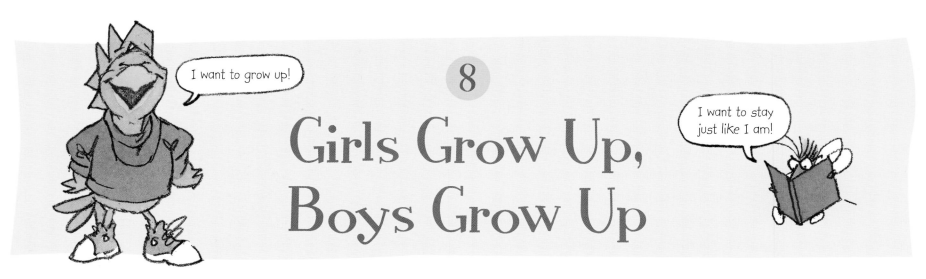

8
Girls Grow Up, Boys Grow Up

When boys and girls grow up, their bodies change and become grown-up bodies. That's when the special parts on the OUTSIDE and INSIDE of their bodies become parts that can help make a baby.

When a girl's body changes, her breasts and hips begin to grow larger. Hair begins to grow under her arms and around her vulva. Her ovaries begin to send out tiny eggs, also called "egg cells."

When a boy's body changes, hair begins to grow on his face, under his arms, next to his penis, and on his chest. His voice begins to sound like a man's voice. His penis and scrotum begin to grow larger. His testicles begin to make very, very tiny sperm, also called "sperm cells."

Wow! Kids grow up to be . . . GROWNUPS!

Well, du-uh! Yes. Kids grow up to be . . . MEN! And kids grow up to be . . . WOMEN!

So Many Eggs! So Many Sperm!

Just two things—one very tiny sperm from inside a man's body and one tiny egg from inside a woman's body—are needed to make a baby.

Every day, millions and millions of very, very tiny sperm are made in a man's testicles. Sperm are so tiny they can only be seen through a microscope.

Here's what sperm look like under a microscope.

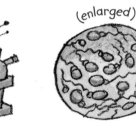

(enlarged)

Boys are born with testicles. But a boy's testicles CANNOT make sperm until his body has become a man's body. That is why boys' bodies cannot make a baby.

Sperm? Like a sperm whale?

Don't think so! These sperm are so tiny! Whales are so huge!

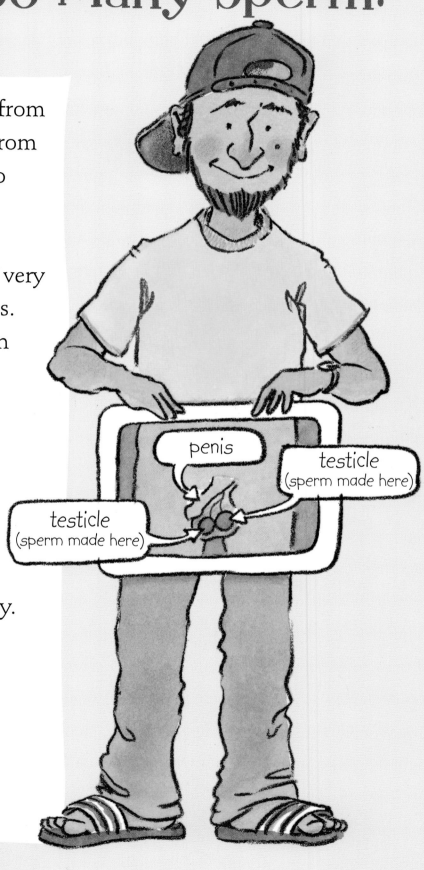

penis

testicle (sperm made here)

testicle (sperm made here)

There are thousands of very tiny eggs in the ovaries. Each egg is about the size of a pencil dot.

(enlarged)

Here's what eggs look like under a microscope.

About once a month, an egg pops out of a woman's ovary and into one of her two Fallopian tubes. Girls are born with eggs in their ovaries. But a girl's eggs ARE NOT READY to make a baby until her body has become a woman's body. That is why girls' bodies cannot make a baby.

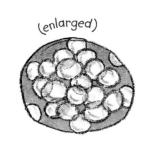

Fallopian tube

uterus

Fallopian tube

ovary
(eggs in here)

ovary
(eggs in here)

Eggs? Like the kind you eat with bacon or sausage??

Don't think so! Those are chicken eggs—not human eggs!

It's NOT the Stork!

To make a baby, a sperm from a man's body and an egg from a woman's body must get together.

1 sperm   1 egg   1 *baby*

When grownups want to make a baby, most often a woman and a man have a special kind of loving called "making love"— "having sex" — or "sex." This kind of loving happens when the woman and the man get so close to each other that the man's penis goes inside the woman's vagina.

Children are much too young to do the special kind of loving—called "sex"— that grownups do.

When grownups have sex, sperm can swim out through the small opening at the tip of the man's penis—and into the woman's vagina. Then the sperm swim through her vagina and through her uterus and into her two Fallopian tubes.

If just one sperm meets and joins together with an egg that's in one of the Fallopian tubes—an amazing thing can happen! The beginning cells of a baby can start to grow!

Sometimes, a sperm and egg are not able to meet inside a woman's body. That's when a doctor can take an egg and a sperm and put them into a little dish where the sperm can swim into the egg. Then the doctor puts the egg inside the woman's uterus and the beginning cells of a baby can start to grow. Or the doctor can put sperm into the woman's vagina, where the sperm swim until they meet an egg in one of her Fallopian tubes.

The BIG Swim

The Growing Womb

The uterus is also called "the womb." Once the ball of cells plants itself in the womb, that's when a woman is "pregnant." "Pregnant" means the woman is going to have a baby. The woman is pregnant until her baby is born. It's hard to believe that a tiny ball of cells can grow into a whole new person—a baby! But it can.

PREGNANT WOMAN
AT THE MOVIES

hungry woman

lemonade

popcorn in the stomach

fetus in the uterus

While a growing baby is inside the uterus, first it is called an "embryo." Then it is called a "fetus" or a "growing baby."

A fetus does not grow in a pregnant woman's stomach. It grows inside her uterus— just below her stomach. The uterus is where a fetus grows until it finally grows into a baby— and is born.

SO the fetus doesn't grow where the popcorn goes!

You got it!

Pinpoint to Watermelon

The ball of cells looks BIG!

(enlarged)

But it's really tiny— as tiny as a pinpoint!

When the tiny ball of cells plants itself inside the uterus, it's called an "embryo." It is about the size of a pinpoint.

It's amazing that in just a few months' time, a tiny fetus grows to be about the size of a watermelon!

1 MONTH By one month, the embryo is about the size of a tomato seed. Its backbone has begun to grow, and its heart has begun to beat.

1 MONTH actual size

1 MONTH (enlarged)

6 MONTHS By six months, the fetus is about the size of a coconut. It can hear and see, kick, punch, hiccup, burp, pee, do somersaults, make noises, hear noises, sleep, and suck its thumb. Its lungs have begun to practice breathing. It has begun to grow eyebrows and eyelashes and can open its eyes. It may have begun to grow hair on its head.

3 MONTHS actual size

6 MONTHS actual size

3 MONTHS By three months, when an embryo becomes a fetus, it is about the size of a large peach. Its arms, fingers, legs, toes, ears, eyes, nose, and lips show. Its fingernails and toenails have begun to grow. Its body has begun to be covered with soft hair to protect it from the water it floats in. And its vagina or penis has also begun to grow.

9 **MONTHS** After growing for nine months— about as long as a school year— the fetus is about the size of a watermelon. Its body may have turned so that its head is facing down. It now has millions of cells, and its brain, heart, lungs, stomach, and other parts of its body are working well. It's ready to be born!

When the fetus grows as big as a watermelon, will the mommy pop?

Hope not!

Is the mommy getting fat?

No-ooo, silly! She's growing a baby in there, silly!

A pregnant woman's uterus does not pop *because* her uterus and her skin are stretchy—like a balloon. While the fetus grows bigger, the woman's uterus and skin stretch. That's why the uterus is a safe place for a fetus to grow.

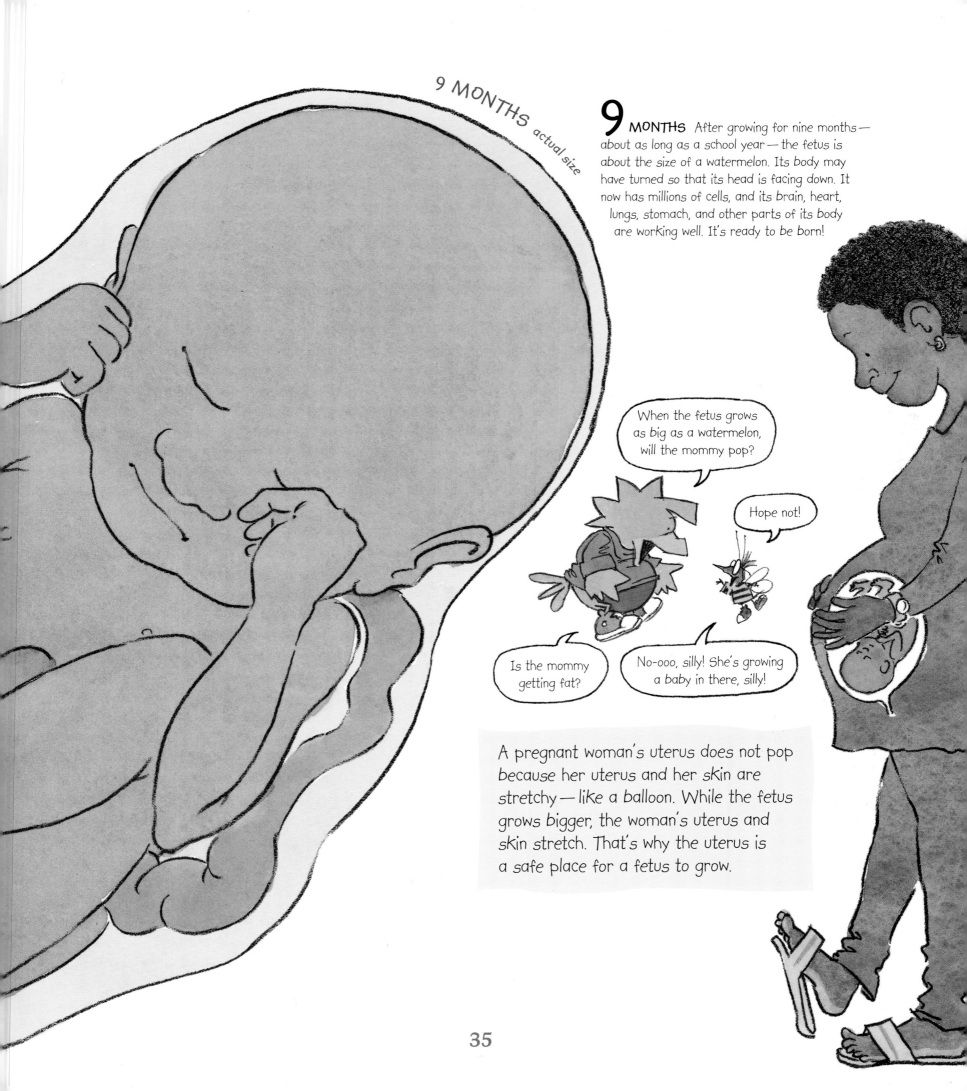

14

The Twisty Cord

A fetus gets the good things it needs to grow and stay healthy from the food a pregnant woman eats and drinks—and from the fresh air she breathes.

The oxygen in the air and bits of food and drink travel from the pregnant woman's body to the fetus through a twisty cord that's attached to the fetus's body. This is the umbilical cord. Your bellybutton is the place where the cord was attached to you when you were growing inside the uterus. "Navel" is another word for bellybutton.

The uterus is filled with warm water. That's what keeps the fetus warm and protects it from bumps and pokes. Sometimes, the fetus drinks the water it floats in and pees a little bit. The fetus's pee leaves a pregnant woman's body with her pee. Most fetuses do not poop inside the uterus.

HOW A FETUS EATS AND BREATHES

1 Fresh air goes into the woman's nose and mouth.

2 Food—like a banana—and drinks—like milk—go into her mouth.

3 Air goes into the woman's two lungs.

4 Food and drinks go through the woman's stomach.

5 Inside her stomach, the food breaks into tiny bits.

6 The bits of food and air travel into the fetus's body through the twisty cord.

SO what does the fetus do all day?

15

All Day, All Night

SO what does the fetus do all night?

While the fetus is growing inside the uterus, it can do so many things! It can kick and punch, do somersaults, suck its thumb and fingers, taste, swallow, blink, stretch, sleep, and make noises— like hiccups and burps.

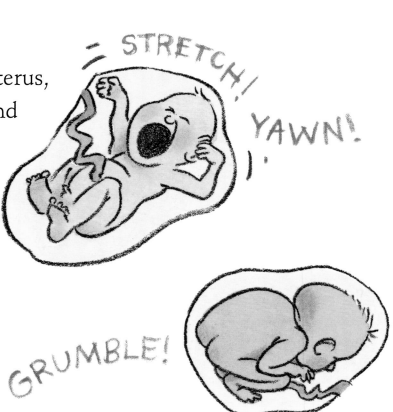

STRETCH! YAWN!

TUMBLE!

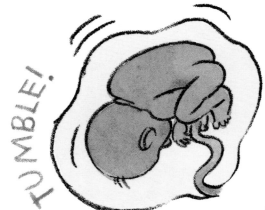

GRUMBLE!

KICK!

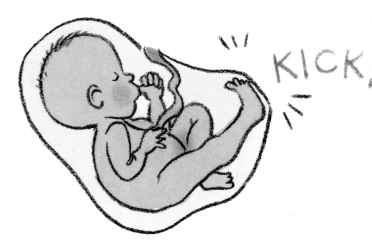

As the fetus grows bigger, it can hear the sound of voices and other noises too — like a doorbell ringing or someone singing. It can hear its mother's heart beating and her stomach grumbling, and it can see bright light.

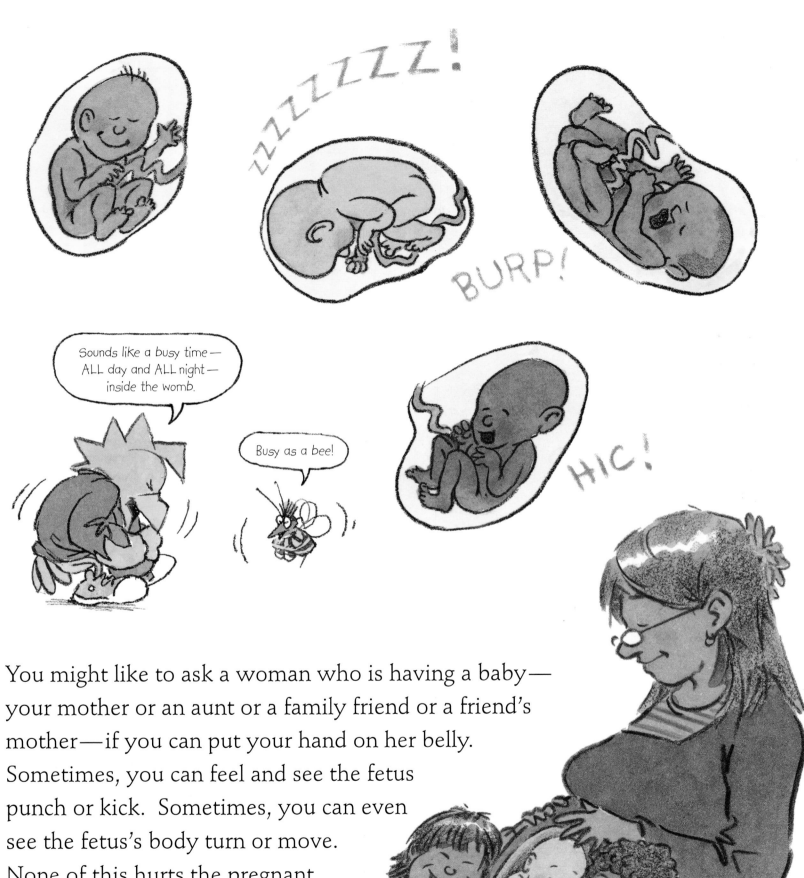

You might like to ask a woman who is having a baby—your mother or an aunt or a family friend or a friend's mother—if you can put your hand on her belly. Sometimes, you can feel and see the fetus punch or kick. Sometimes, you can even see the fetus's body turn or move. None of this hurts the pregnant woman or the fetus.

Boy? Girl? 1 Baby? 2 or More?

How do you know if the baby is going to be a boy or a girl or —

one baby or more?

When a doctor or nurse takes a moving computer picture of the fetus inside the uterus—called an "ultrasound"—sometimes you can see the fetus moving, punching, kicking, or sleeping. Sometimes you can see if the fetus has a penis. If it does, it will be born a boy. If it doesn't, it has a vulva and will be born a girl. That's how some families know before their baby is born whether it will be born a boy or a girl.

Some families choose not to look and find out if their baby will be born a girl or a boy. They want to be surprised. They wait until the baby is born to find out. Some families bring home a computer picture of the fetus to show to the rest of their family and to their friends.

When a doctor or nurse takes a computer picture, they can also find out if a pregnant woman has one, two, or even more fetuses growing inside her uterus.

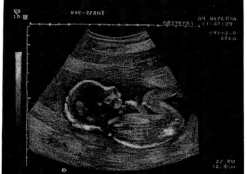

COMPUTER PICTURE OF A FETUS

Wow! A computer can see inside my body!

I don't want to see inside ANYBODY!

Usually only one fetus is growing in the uterus.
Sometimes there are two, three, or more.

If there are two fetuses, two babies—
twins—will be born. If there are three,
triplets will be born. If there are four,
quadruplets will be born. If there are
five, quintuplets will be born.

Some twins, triplets, quadruplets, and
quintuplets look exactly like each other.
Some do not. Twins, triplets, quadruplets,
and quintuplets can be all boys or all
girls—or boys and girls.

It's a Baby!

Most babies are born in a hospital. Some babies are born at home. Most times special people — doctors or midwives, nurses or doulas — help the mommy while her baby is being born. Often the daddy, or the partner, or sometimes aunts, uncles, grandparents, or good friends, also help.

When a baby is ready to be born, the muscles inside the mommy's uterus push the baby out of the uterus and through the mommy's vagina. The vagina stretches to make room for the baby as it slides out — and is born! Most babies are born this way.

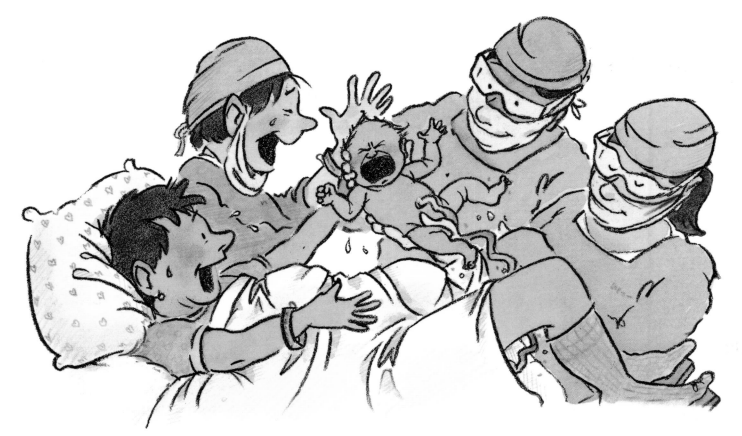

Another way a baby is born is when the doctor makes a cut through the mommy's skin and into her uterus. The mommy is given a special medicine before the cutting so that it won't hurt. After the cutting, the baby is lifted out of the uterus— and is born! Then the cut is sewed up with a special thread. Many babies are born this way. This kind of birth is called a cesarean birth or a c-section. You might like to ask your parent which way you were born and if you were born at a hospital or at home.

I pecked my way out of my eggshell. That's how I was born.

I hatched out of my egg. That's how I was born.

BZZZZZZZZzzzzz

The moment a baby is born, someone often shouts out, "IT'S A GIRL!" or "IT'S A BOY!"— even if the parent or parents already knew the baby would be a girl or boy. The moment a baby is born is so exciting!

It's a BABY!

Happy Birthday!

Happy Birthday to YOU!

Happy Birthday to YOU!

WHAAAAAAAAA!!

Most babies let out a cry the moment they are born. That's how a baby begins to breathe on his or her own. As soon as the baby is born, the twisty cord that attached the growing baby to its mommy is cut. The cutting does not hurt the baby or the mommy.

The cord is cut because now the baby can breathe air on its own. And now the new baby can drink with its mouth from its mommy's breasts or from a bottle. Milk from the mommy's breasts or special milk from a bottle is all the food a new baby needs.

My family was so happy to see me and cuddle me and call me "Sweetie Birdy"!

The place where the cord was attached becomes the baby's bellybutton. As soon as the cord is cut—and sometimes even before—the baby's parent or parents can finally hold and cuddle and kiss the new baby. It feels so wonderful to hold and look at the new baby!

My family was so happy to see me and cuddle me and call me "Honeybunch"!

The day you were born was your "birth day" and that never changes. The word "birth" means "the beginning of something new" or "a new baby." Each year on your birthday, everyone loves to sing "Happy Birthday!" to you because they are so excited and happy that you were born.

19
Cuddles and Kisses

All babies do is cry, sleep, pee, poop — and take baths too.

That's okay. Kids and grownups do these things too.

Most kids and grownups can't remember being a baby. You might want to ask your parent or parents to show you pictures of yourself when you were little. Or you could ask them to tell you stories about all the amazing things you could do and what you were like when you were little.

If you watch a new baby, you'll see that new babies can do lots of things. They often get tired because they are doing so many new things. That's why they sleep a lot—and cry a lot.

Babies cry when they are tired or hungry. They also cry when they have peed or pooped and need a dry diaper.

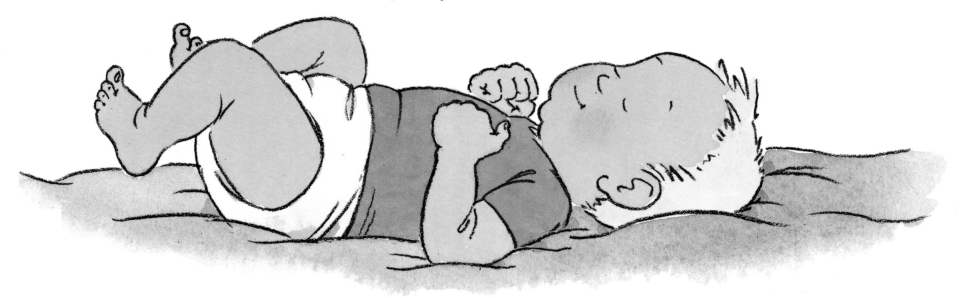

When babies are hungry, they can suck and drink special milk from their mommy's breasts or from a bottle. Babies cry when they need a cuddle and kiss or when they are too hot or too cold. Crying is one of the ways babies tell us what they want and how they feel.

Babies are crybabies.

Crying is okay—even if you're not a baby.

Even though new babies can see and hear and gurgle, they need other people—their mommy, or daddy, or uncle, or aunt, grandparent, caregiver, or babysitter—to take care of them. An older brother or sister or cousin can help change a diaper, help give a bath, and when babies are older—help feed them. They can also play games with the baby—like "Peekaboo! I Love You!"

Babies also love to be cuddled, kissed, smiled at, talked to, and sung to by older sisters and brothers and cousins. Babies love to be with older kids!

All Kinds of Families

I have a very nice family!

I have a very sweet family!

Almost all babies grow up in and are loved and taken care of by a family. Most babies are born into their family. Some babies and children are adopted into their family.

Some families have one child. Some families have two, or three, or four, or more children. Some families have a mommy and a daddy. Some have a mommy. Some have a daddy. Some have two mommies. Some have two daddies. Some kids live with a parent and stepparent, or with an aunt, an uncle, a grandmother, or grandfather, or with a foster parent. Some kids live with one parent part of the time and with their other parent the rest of the time.

Sometimes, a parent or parents cannot take care of their baby or child. So they make a plan for their baby or child to be adopted—to become part of another family. And that baby or child lives with, grows up with, and is loved and taken care of by the parent or parents who adopt them. And the baby or child becomes part of that parent's or parents' family. When that happens, that's called "adoption."

Parents, sisters, brothers, cousins, aunts, uncles, and grandparents are all part of a person's family. And for many people, good friends, babysitters, and nannies are part of their families too.

Adoption's an awesome way to be a family!

And there are so many awesome kinds of families!

Okay Touches, Not Okay Touches

Babies, kids, teenagers, and grownups all need cuddles and hugs and kisses from the people who are good to us and love us. The everyday hugs and kisses and touching and holding hands with our families and good friends are "okay touches." There are "okay touches" and "NOT okay touches."

The parts of our bodies that are under our underpants or bathing suits are called "privates" or "our privates." If you touch or rub the private parts of your own body because it tickles and feels good, that's an "okay touch."

Well, "my privates" are under my feathers.

Well, my whole body is private — and that's THAT!

During a checkup, the reason your doctor or nurse has to look at and touch "your privates" is to make sure that every part of your body is healthy. This kind of touching done by a doctor or nurse is also an "okay touch."

If any person touches "your privates" or any other part of your body that you do not want them to—these are all "not okay touches." If this happens to you, tell that person "STOP!" or "NO!" or "DON'T!" — even if the person is someone in your family, or a friend, or someone you know or you love—or is bigger, older, or stronger than you are.

I'm very small, you know.

But big enough to say "NO!" "STOP!" or "DON'T!"

If any kind of "not okay touch" happens to you, tell a grownup right away—even if the person who touched you tells you to keep it a secret. This is a secret you have to tell someone.

Tell someone in your family, or your teacher, or doctor, or nurse, or school nurse, or someone you know very well. If the first person you tell does not help you or believe you, keep on telling people until someone believes you. That person will do everything she or he can to help keep you safe and protect you and to make the "not okay touches" stop. Luckily, there are many grownups who can and will help.

Talking about this is scary. . . .

Talking about this makes me feel better. . . . Need a hug?

I do . . . my friend.

Here's a NOT-too-tight hug, my friend.

Girls, Boys, Friends

As you grow up from a baby to a little kid to a big kid—it's fun to have a friend. It doesn't matter how many friends you have, or if your friends are boys, or girls, or girls and boys. What matters most is being a good friend.

Taking turns, sharing a toy, or playing a game together are great ways to be a good friend. Being nice when a friend feels bad or sad or mad is another way to be a good friend.

Saying "I'm sorry!" is also a way to be a good friend. So is holding hands, giving a hug, or just talking with a friend.

SO-OOO what's a girlfriend—and a boyfriend?

That's when teenagers get all smoochy and all lovey-dovey. And some grownups have girlfriends and boyfriends. But we just have friends.

Anytime you do not want to hold hands, or be touched, or hugged, or kissed by a friend—it's okay to tell a friend that. Or if a friend does not want to hold hands, or be touched or hugged, or kissed by you, that's okay too. Good friends listen to each other.

I don't want to do THAT!

Okay.

If a friend asks you to do something you don't want to do or think you shouldn't do—like climbing too high, or teasing someone, or taking off your clothes—you can say, "No, I won't do that!" or "I don't want to do that"—even if your friends tell you it's okay to do it.

You don't have to do everything a friend tells or asks you to do. Friends do not have to do everything you tell them to do. It's also okay for friends to do different things— and even get mad at each other. No matter what, it's so nice to have a friend.

Glad you are my friend, my friend.

Whew! Glad to hear that, my friend.

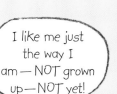

Growing Up

You are growing up! Once you were a baby. Now you are a kid. One day you will be a teenager. It's hard to believe, but someday you will be a grownup. You might even decide to be a mommy or a daddy. And when you are even older, you may become a grandpa or a grandma!

When girls and boys grow up, some grow up to be women and some grow up to be men. Growing up from a baby to a kid to a teenager to a grownup takes a long time and a lot of years.

is so amazing!

Bee-lieve It!

Thank You!

THANK YOU to ALL these people who helped with this book!

And ALL these people care about children and families! So THANK YOU ALL!

TINA ALU, family planning director, Cambridge Economic Opportunity Committee, Cambridge, Massachusetts

BETSY ANDERSON, Kindergarten teacher, Shady Hill School, Cambridge, Massachusetts

SARAH BIRSS, M.D., pediatrician/child psychiatrist, Cambridge, Massachusetts

DEBORAH CHAMBERLAIN, research associate, Norwood, Massachusetts

NANCY CLOSE, PH.D., assistant professor, Yale University Child Study Center, New Haven, Connecticut

SALLY CRISSMAN, science educator, Watertown, Massachusetts

MARY DOMINGUEZ, elementary science educator, Belmont Public Schools, Belmont, Massachusetts

BEN H. HARRIS, parent, New York, New York

BILL HARRIS, grandparent, Cambridge, Massachusetts

DAVID B. HARRIS, parent, New York, New York

EMILY B. HARRIS, parent, New York, New York

HILARY G. HARRIS, parent, New York, New York

ROBYN HEILBRUN, grandparent, Salt Lake City, Utah

CARLA HORWITZ, ED.D., director, Calvin Hill Day Care Center; Kindergarten lecturer, Yale University Child Study Center and Department of Psychology, New Haven, Connecticut

LESLIE KANTOR, M.P.H., director of education, Planned Parenthood of New York City, New York, New York

JILL KANTROWITZ, director of education, Planned Parenthood League of Massachusetts, Boston, Massachusetts

MARGOT KAPLAN-SANOFF, ED.D., infant and child development specialist, Head Start Training and Technical Assistance Quality Initiative, Boston, Massachusetts

ELLEN KELLEY, early childhood consultant, Arlington, Massachusetts

SALLY LESSER, bookseller, Cambridge, Massachusetts

AMY LEVINE, family project coordinator, Sexuality Information and Education Council of the United States, New York, New York

ELIZABETH A. LEVY, children's book author, New York, New York

ALICIA F. LIEBERMAN, PH.D., professor of medical psychology, University of California at San Francisco, San Francisco, California

CAROL LYNCH, M.ED., sexuality educator, Arlington, Massachusetts

STEVEN MARANS, PH.D., professor of child psychiatry and psychiatry, Yale University Child Study Center, New Haven, Connecticut

WENDY DALTON MARANS, M.SC., associate research scientist, Yale University Child Study Center, New Haven, Connecticut

LINDA C. MAYES, M.D., Arnold Gesell professor of child psychiatry, pediatrics, and psychology, Yale University Child Study Center, New Haven, Connecticut; co-chairman of directorial team, Anna Freud Centre, London, UK

MICHAEL McGEE, vice president for education, Planned Parenthood Federation of America, New York, New York

ELI NEWBERGER, M.D., senior associate in medicine, Children's Hospital; assistant professor of pediatrics, Harvard Medical School, Boston, Massachusetts

JANET PATTERSON, M.ED., librarian, Advent School, Boston, Massachusetts

LAURA RILEY, M.D., obstetrician/gynecologist, director, OB/GYN Infectious Diseases, Massachusetts General Hospital, Boston, Massachusetts

MONICA RODRIQUEZ, vice president for education and training, Sexuality Information and Education Council of the United States, New York, New York

HEATHER Z. SANKEY, M.D., obstetrician/gynecologist, residency program director, Baystate Medical Center, Springfield, Massachusetts

KAREN SHORR, M.A.T., preKindergarten teacher, The Brookwood School, Manchester, Massachusetts

VICTORIA SOLOMON, children's librarian, Cambridge Public Library, Cambridge, Massachusetts

SUSAN WEBBER, consultant, Arlington, Massachusetts

ELAINE WINTER, M.ED., lower school principal, Little Red School House, New York, New York

MARY YOUNG, M.ED., assistant director of early childhood admissions, early childhood learning specialist, Little Red School House, New York, New York

PAMELA M. ZUCKERMAN, M.D., pediatrician, Brookline, Massachusetts

And a giant thanks to everyone at Candlewick Press, especially to MARY LEE DONOVAN and CAROLINE LAWRENCE for understanding and supporting our vision, to ANDREA TOMPA for keeping track of everything, and to EMIL FORTUNE and LUCY INGRAMS at Walker Books UK for making sure our books work for children and families across the big pond.

Index

First paperback edition 2008

The Library of Congress has cataloged the hardcover edition as follows:

Harris, Robie H.
It's not the stork! : a book about girls, boys, babies, bodies, families, and friends /
Robie H. Harris ; illustrated by Michael Emberley.
p.   cm.
ISBN 978-0-7636-0047-1 (hardcover)
1. Sex instruction for children. 2. Sex role in children—Juvenile literature.
3. Sex differences—Juvenile literature. 4. Childbirth—Juvenile literature.
I. Emberley, Michael. II. Title.
HQ53.H36 2006
649'.65—dc22   2005054280

ISBN 978-0-7636-3331-8 (paperback)

17 18 19 20 CCP 20 19

Printed in Shenzhen, Guangdong, China

This book was typeset in Stempel Schneidler.
The illustrations were done in colored pencil and watercolor.

Candlewick Press
99 Dover Street
Somerville, Massachusetts 02144

visit us at www.candlewick.com

Praise from the Experts for *It's NOT the Stork!*

"*It's Not the Stork!* is both captivating and encyclopedic, covering in great detail not only sexual reproduction but also the joys of love (in its many forms), the mysteries of pregnancy, and the miracle of birth. This book explains the gender differences that children are already wondering about, affirming their need to be curious. It will leave them, and their parents, better informed, and still more in awe of nature's wondrous ways."

—T. Berry Brazelton, M.D., and Joshua D. Sparrow, M.D., authors of *Touchpoints, Three to Six: Your Child's Emotional and Behavioral Development* and The Brazelton Way series

"Children have great curiosity about the differences between the sexes and how babies are made—they will appreciate *It's Not the Stork!* immensely. I strongly recommend it."

— Alvin F. Poussaint, M.D., Professor of Psychiatry, Harvard Medical School and Judge Baker Children's Center, Boston; co-author of *Raising Black Children*

"We recommend Harris and Emberley's sensitive, level-headed, and delightful books wherever we go. Now, with the arrival of *It's Not the Stork!*, even children as young as four can benefit from this team's honest answers to the questions that make parents blush."

—Justin Richardson, M.D., and Mark A. Schuster, M.D., Ph.D., authors of *Everything You Never Wanted Your Kids to Know about Sex (but Were Afraid They'd Ask)*

"Young children are talkative and curious about everything, including their bodies, their gender, and their birth. I highly recommend *It's Not the Stork!* for libraries in homes, schools, and faith communities."

—The Reverend Patricia Hoertdoerfer, Unitarian Universalist Association

"Robie Harris and Michael Emberley have done it again! They understand the complexity, the humor, and the urgency of young children's curiosity about bodies and babies and the whole great mystery of life, and they offer clear words and delightful illustrations to help parents enjoy the process of helping their children learn and understand. This is a book for adults and young children to enjoy together, offering age-appropriate, sensible, friendly information in a way that will inform, reassure, and even amuse."

—Perri Klass, M.D., Associate Professor of Pediatrics, Boston University School of Medicine; pediatrician, Dorchester House, Boston; and contributing editor, *Parenting* Magazine

"Finally, a reassuring book for our young children (age four and up) who are wondering about or asking about how they were made and what it is that makes them a girl or a boy. The simple, clear, and straightforward language, along with the accurate and appealing cartoon-like illustrations, answer these questions in an honest and comforting way, while celebrating the diversity of our times."

—Angela Diaz, M.D., M.P.H., Professor of Pediatrics and Community Medicine, Mount Sinai School of Medicine, and director, Mount Sinai Adolescent Health Center, New York City

"*It's Not the Stork!* gives the younger crowd the gentle truth before being exposed to scary playground fantasy. Please don't scoff or squirm! Even our youngest children notice, wonder, and need to know who they are, where they came from, how they got here, and what makes them the same or not the same as their friends. But not all parents know just what to tell and when and how. This book does!"

—Penelope Leach, Ph.D., author of *Your Baby & Child* and contributing editor, *Child* Magazine

Here's what people are saying about the series

Let's Talk About **YOU** and **ME**

"The simple words and pictures help parents answer young children's questions clearly and comfortably." – **T. Berry Brazelton**, **MD**, founder of the Brazelton Touchpoints Center, Children's Hospital, Boston, and **Joshua Sparrow**, **MD**, co-authors of *Touchpoints: Birth to Three* and *Touchpoints: Three to Six*

"Will answer questions, start conversations, and make everyone smile." – **Perri Klass**, **MD**, Professor of Journalism and Pediatrics, New York University; Director of Graduate Studies, Arthur L. Carter Journalism Institute

Check out all the books in the series

Who Has What?
ALL About Girls' Bodies and Boys' Bodies
ROBIE H. HARRIS
illustrated by NADINE BERNARD WESTCOTT

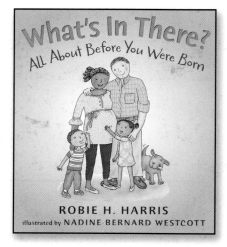

What's In There?
ALL About Before You Were Born
ROBIE H. HARRIS
illustrated by NADINE BERNARD WESTCOTT

Who's In My Family?
ALL About Our Families
ROBIE H. HARRIS
illustrated by NADINE BERNARD WESTCOTT

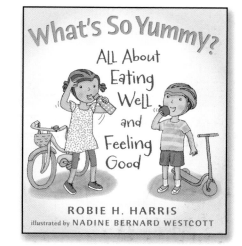

What's So Yummy?
ALL About Eating Well and Feeling Good
ROBIE H. HARRIS
illustrated by NADINE BERNARD WESTCOTT

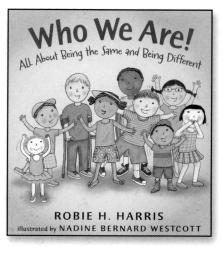

Who We Are!
ALL About Being the Same and Being Different
ROBIE H. HARRIS
illustrated by NADINE BERNARD WESTCOTT